ed on or before

I didn't know that

some bugs glow in the dark

© Aladdin Books Ltd 1997
Produced by
Aladdin Books Ltd
28 Percy Street
London W1P 0LD

ISBN 0-7496-2700-X
First published in Great Britain in 1997 by
Aladdin Books /Watts Books
96 Leonard Street
London EC2A 4RH

Concept, editorial and design by

David West   Children's Books

Designer: Robert Perry
Illustrators: Myke Taylor, Rob Shone and Jo Moore

Printed in Belgium

I didn't know that some bugs glow in the dark

Claire Llewellyn

A l a d d i n / W a t t s

London • Sydney

I didn't know that

Introduction

Did *you* know that
you would need to use
dynamite to blow up
a termite's home?
... that stick insects
can grow as long as
a cat?

... that some wasps lay their eggs in pots?
Discover for yourself amazing
facts about the insect world, from
the tiniest fairy fly and the high-
jumping flea to the insect that
eats birds...

Look out for
this symbol
which means there
is a fun project for
you to try.

Is it true or is it
false? Watch for this
symbol and try to answer
the question before
reading on for the answer.

Don't forget to check the borders for extra amazing facts.

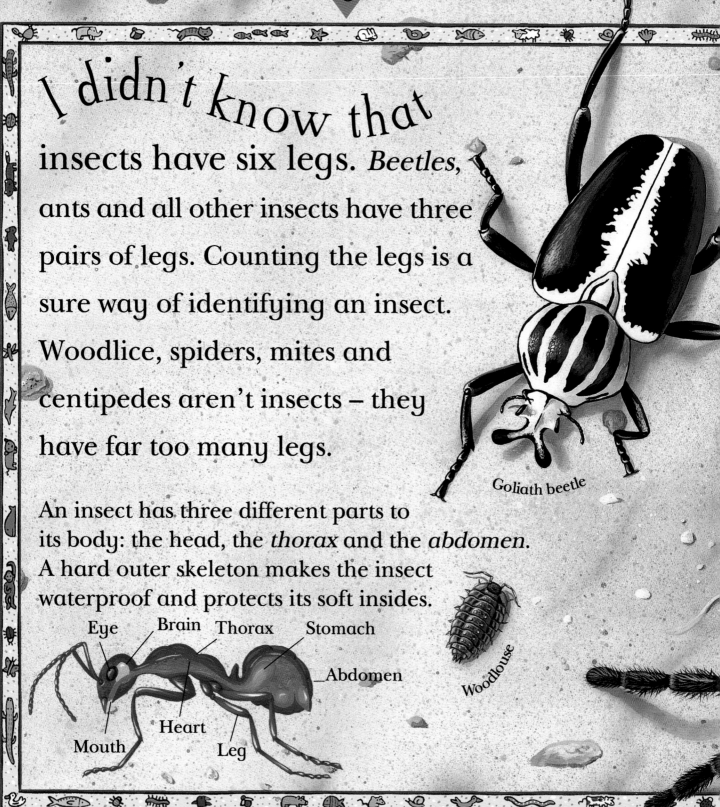

I didn't know that

insects have six legs. *Beetles*, ants and all other insects have three pairs of legs. Counting the legs is a sure way of identifying an insect. Woodlice, spiders, mites and centipedes aren't insects – they have far too many legs.

An insect has three different parts to its body: the head, the *thorax* and the *abdomen*. A hard outer skeleton makes the insect waterproof and protects its soft insides.

Goliath beetle

Eye Brain Thorax Stomach

Abdomen

Mouth Heart Leg

Woodlouse

The first insects lived 370 million years ago - long before the dinosaurs.

FIND & SEARCH & FIND & SEARCH & FIND

Find one insect and three imposters.

People who study insects are called entomologists. They learn about insects, how and where they live and how best to protect them.

Centipede

There are well over a million kinds of insects in the world. That's more than all the other kinds of animals put together! Entomologists discover 8,000 new insects every year.

Bird-eating spider

7

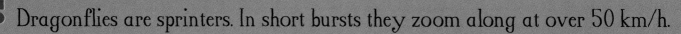

True or false?
Flies have only one pair of wings.

Answer: **True**

Flies that have one pair of wings, such as the housefly, are called true flies. Dragonflies and mayflies have two pairs of wings, so they're not true flies at all. Beetles have one pair of wings but their *wingcases* count as a second pair – so beetles are not true flies either!

Beetle

A wasp's second pair of wings is hard to see.

Bluebottle

SEARCH & FIND & SEARCH & FIND

Can you find five true flies?

Wasp

I didn't know that

beetles can fly. Ladybirds and many other beetles can all fly when they need to. They open up the wingcases on their back, unfold their soft wings and take off!

Dragonfly

Butterfly

Flying insects survive tropical storms because the raindrops make a breeze as they fall, which blows tiny insects aside. They end up flying between the drops.

A butterfly's wings are covered with rows of scales, arranged like the tiles on a roof. Each scale is like a tiny speck of dust.

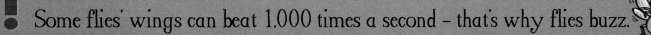

Some flies' wings can beat 1,000 times a second – that's why flies buzz.

I didn't know that

caterpillars are baby butterflies. Like many insects, butterflies change completely as they grow – from an egg, to a caterpillar, to a *pupa*, to a butterfly. This way of growing is called *metamorphosis.*

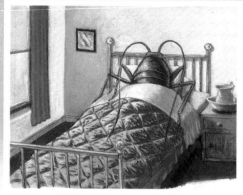

The Austrian writer Franz Kafka, wrote a book called Metamorphosis. It's about a man who changed into a giant insect.

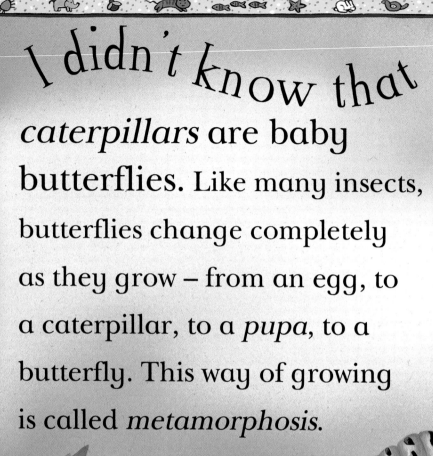

SEARCH & FIND

Can you find nine caterpillars?

FIND & SEARCH

Not all insects change as they grow. Baby shield bugs look like their parents when they hatch. They just get bigger and bigger, and eventually grow their wings.

Mayflies spend most of their lives as wingless *larvae*. Once they change into adult mayflies, they only live for a day.

Some caterpillars change into moths, not butterflies.

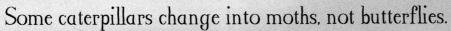

I didn't know that

some bugs can walk on water. Pondskaters are so light that they can skim across ponds without falling into the water. Hairy tufts on their tiny feet help them to stay afloat.

SEARCH & FIND
Can you find the water snail?
FIND & SEARCH

Pondskater

Dragonfly nymph

Dragonflies begin life in water as creatures called *nymphs*. They will attack small fish and tadpoles that are bigger than themselves.

Tadpole

A water boatman lies on its back and rows through the water.

river beach

True or false?
Water beetles in lakes and ponds can breathe under the water.

Water beetle

Answer: **False**

Water beetles can't breathe under water. They swim to the surface to collect air bubbles. These supply them with air when they dive under water.

The Ancient Greeks and Romans believed that beautiful nature goddesses lived in rivers and streams. They were called water nymphs.

13

I didn't know that

termite mounds have air conditioning. Termites build themselves tall mud towers, where millions of the insects live. Every tower has a chimney which draws up warm air and keeps the nest cool.

Tropical weaver ants build their homes out of leaves. Some of the ants hold the leaves together, while others stick them with a sticky glue. The glue comes from larvae the ants carry in their jaws.

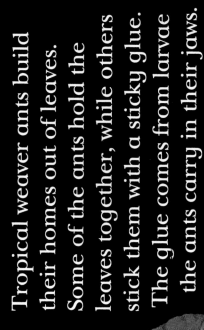

SEARCH & FIND
Can you find the queen termite?

1

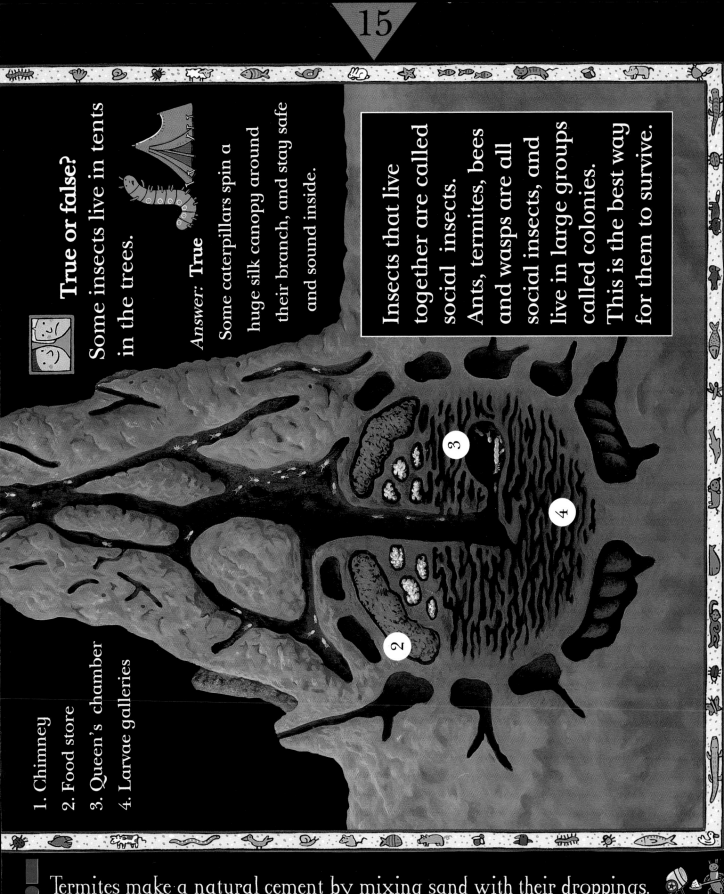

True or false?

Some insects live in tents in the trees.

Answer: **True**

Some caterpillars spin a huge silk canopy around their branch, and stay safe and sound inside.

Insects that live together are called social insects. Ants, termites, bees and wasps are all social insects, and live in large groups called colonies. This is the best way for them to survive.

1. Chimney
2. Food store
3. Queen's chamber
4. Larvae galleries

Termites make a natural cement by mixing sand with their droppings.

Potter wasp

In Ancient Egypt, the dung beetle was the symbol for the Sun god, who rolled the Sun across the sky each day.

I didn't know that some wasps build pots. The female potter wasp makes tiny mud pots, and lays an egg in each one. Before sealing a pot, she pokes a *grub* inside – a tasty meal for her young when it hatches.

Dung beetle brooch from Ancient Egypt

Most insects don't make nests. They just lay their eggs near some food.

 True or false?

Insects make bad parents. They never look after their young.

Answer: **False**

The female fungus beetle cleans and protects her eggs until they hatch. Then she helps the larvae to feed for about two weeks.

Fungus beetle

Dung beetles lay their eggs inside balls of dung – their larvae's favourite food. The beetles make the balls by rolling bits of dung along the ground.

You can make a giant potter wasp's pot. Roll damp clay into thin ropes, and coil them in circles to make a jar. Copy the shape from the picture (above left). Be sure to make a lip around the top. Smooth the sides and leave it to dry.

17

True or false?

A honey bee tastes its food with its feet.

Answer: **True**

A honey bee tastes with its feet as well as its mouth. It can sample its food as soon as it lands on it. So can houseflies.

Proboscis

Butterflies suck up the *nectar* from flowers through a long tongue called a proboscis. When they're not feeding, they keep it curled up out of the way.

Cockroaches eat anything – meat, bread, fruit, cardboard...

I didn't know that

ants are great farmers.
Just as farmers keep cows, so some kinds of ants keep *aphids*. They protect them from their enemies, and in return the ants 'milk' the aphids for the honeydew they suck up.

SEARCH & FIND
Can you find the bumble bee?
FIND & SEARCH

If you want to study moths you can attract them by leaving a mixture of sugar and water near a lighted, open window at night.

19

I didn't know that

some insects eat lizards.

When a praying mantis snaps its spiny legs, its helpless prey is trapped inside. Mantises are fierce hunters. Most of them eat other insects, but some catch lizards and frogs.

Praying mantis

A female mantis is so dangerous, she'll even eat her mate.

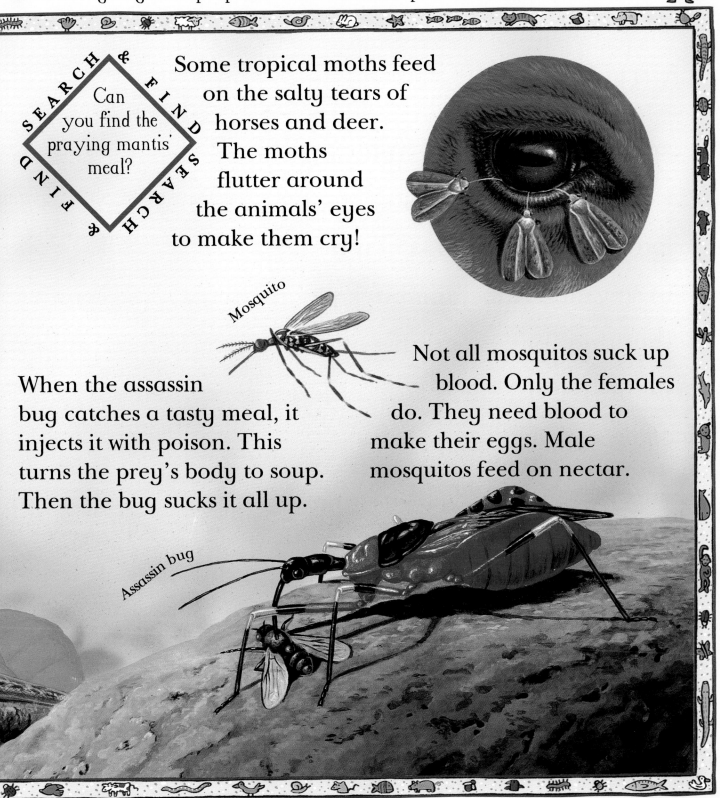

SEARCH & FIND SEARCH & FIND SEARCH & FIND

Can you find the praying mantis' meal?

Some tropical moths feed on the salty tears of horses and deer. The moths flutter around the animals' eyes to make them cry!

Mosquito

When the assassin bug catches a tasty meal, it injects it with poison. This turns the prey's body to soup. Then the bug sucks it all up.

Not all mosquitos suck up blood. Only the females do. They need blood to make their eggs. Male mosquitos feed on nectar.

Assassin bug

I didn't know that

some leaves are insects.
Leaf insects look just like the
leaves they feed on. They blend
in so well against the background
that their enemies don't often see
them. This is called *camouflage*.

Many animals eat caterpillars,
but the hawkmoth caterpillar
has a clever disguise to frighten
its enemies away. It looks just
like a hungry snake!

Leaf insect

Stick insect

Hawkmoth caterpillar

22

These fly orchids aren't insects at all but plants that mimic insects. They look like female insects. This attracts the male insects to them which can then pollinate (fertilise) them.

Camouflage isn't only for defence. The pink flower mantis is brilliantly hidden inside an orchid – the better to ambush its prey.

When thorn bugs land on twigs, they look like nasty prickles. And even if they're caught, they're much too sharp to eat.

Flower mantis

Thorn bugs

! Many insects are green so they match the leaves they feed on.

I didn't know that

some insects stink. Stink bugs are the skunks of the insect world. When they're frightened, they let out a dreadful smell from tiny holes between their legs. This gets rid of enemies – fast!

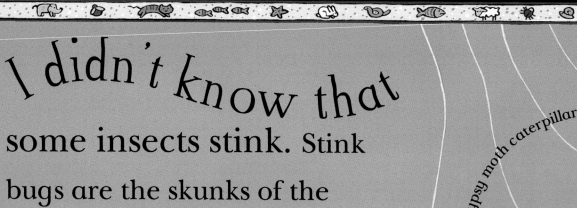

Gypsy moth caterpillars

Gypsy moth caterpillars escape danger by dropping down on a line of silk and wafting away on the wind.

Stink bugs

SEARCH & FIND

Can you find five small stink bugs?

The wetapunga is a huge *cricket* with long legs covered in spikes. When it's caught by a bird, the weta kicks out for all it's worth, and is usually dropped in surprise!

Wetapunga

A bombardier beetle fires at its enemies with a boiling hot jet of chemicals. It really stings!

Bombardier beetle

True or false?
You could read by the light of a glow-worm.

Answer: **True**
Glow-worms were once used as reading lamps. Their glow lasts two hours or more.

I didn't know that

some bugs glow in the dark.

To find a mate, female fireflies make a light in their abdomen and flash signals to males. They are called glow-worms.

An insect's feelers aren't just for feeling. They help it to pick up smells in the air – and tastes and sounds, too.

SEARCH & FIND
FIND & SEARCH
Can you find the imposter?

A red mite is not an insect. It has eight legs.

When an ant finds some food, it marks the path to it with a strong-smelling scent. Other ants soon follow the scent, and turn up to share the feast.

500 years ago, rat fleas were the most dangerous insects in the world. They spread a deadly sickness called the plague, which killed millions and millions of people.

When the Queen Alexandra birdwing butterfly spreads its wings, it measures 28 cm from wingtip to wingtip. No wonder it's mistaken for a bird.

Fleas can jump an incredible 130 times their own height.

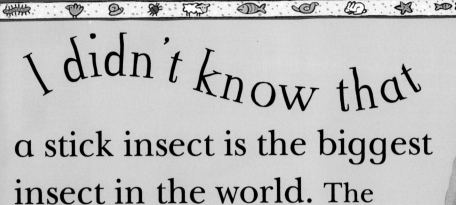

I didn't know that

a stick insect is the biggest insect in the world. The Indonesian giant stick insect measures over 30 cm from tip to toe. It's so big that it moves very slowly.

SEARCH & FIND SEARCH & FIND Can you find ten fairy flies?

It's difficult to see real fairy flies – they are the size of a pinprick.

Male cicadas are the loudest insects in the world. Their clicking noise can be heard by females a kilometre away.

Glossary

Abdomen
The last of the three parts of an insect's body.

Aphids
Tiny insects, such as greenflies, that feed by sucking up the juices from plants.

Beetles
A group of insects that have hard wingcases and can usually fly.

Camouflage
The colours and markings on an insect which help it to blend in with its surroundings and make it difficult to see.

Caterpillar
The larva of a moth or butterfly.

Crickets
A group of insects that are related to grasshoppers, and make a loud chirping noise.

Grub
The young caterpillar-like stage of a beetle and some other insects.

Larva (*plural*: larvae)
The young stage of an insect before metamorphosis. Caterpillars, maggots and grubs are all types of larvae.

Metamorphosis
The change from the young stage to the adult stage of an insect. Many insects change from a larva, to a pupa, to a fully-grown adult.

Nectar
The sweet liquid inside flowers, which attracts insects and other animals.

Nymph
The young stage of an insect that hatches looking just like its parents.

Pupa
The stage in an insect's life when it develops inside a hard, protective case.

Queen
The only egg-laying female in a nest of social insects, such as termites and bees.

Thorax
The middle part of an insect's body, between the head and the abdomen.

Wingcases
Hard outer wings that are not used for flying.

Index